The Great Life Planner

**An easy guide to experiencing
more love, more energy and more fun**

Janine Lattimore

Contents

Step 2: Harmonise (51)

Step 3: Prioritise (61)

Step 4: Actualise (65)

Appendices

Introduction

Reduce stress, do less, and receive more

This book is designed to help you focus your thoughts and energy in an enjoyable way to empower you to create the fulfilling and successful life you desire.

Living in this way does take a foundational mindset shift from focusing on doing and getting things, to focusing on how you feel. That is not to say getting and having things such as a stylish car, a great romantic partner, tropical island holidays or your own beautiful home isn't great and totally possible. However, it isn't actually the things themselves you really want. What you really want is how you think you will feel in having the things. What you really want is to feel happy, loved, successful, safe, supported, abundant, free etc.

Living a ridiculously great life doesn't come from your accomplishments, nice as they are, nor your relationships, however filled with love, nor from how much money you have…it comes from the quality of the feelings that you live in on a daily basis.

Author Elle Sommer

Although we live in a seemingly physical reality, everything is really energy vibrating at a particular frequency. We accept that in terms of things like light, sound and electricity, but it is also true of solid things like rocks and tables, and human beings. For example, the human nervous system uses electricity to send signals throughout the body and brain so that we can think, feel and move. We can use an electroencephalogram (EEG) to measure electrical activity in the brain. Our thoughts and feelings are electrochemical energy.

Normal goal setting focuses on the physical; on doing and getting things. The problem with this, is that many people find that even when they do get the things they thought they wanted, they don't feel happy or satisfied. Often people get so focused on getting things like a job promotion, a better home, or finishing a project, so focused on the end outcome, that they lose sight of why they wanted it in the first place and what is truly important to them. Moreover, the journey to achieving traditional goals is often one of grind, struggle and sacrifice. That isn't really a fulfilling way to live.

I'm inviting you to try a new way of creating a great life, one that allows you to feel good while you are moving forward into more of what you want. In fact, feeling good is pretty much what makes the whole process work.

We're going to swap goals for intentions, timeframes for priorities, and things for feelings (but don't worry, you'll still get to have surprisingly, wonderful things). First up though, let's explore the mindset needed to create this shift.

Living with Intention

When we don't choose a focus, we become swept up in the demands of the people and environment around us, which leads to stress, overwhelm and feelings of not being in control.

Living a Reactive Life versus Living a Created Life

You can either live life by reacting to what is going on outside of you, or you can live life by initiating and creating what you want. I call this living a Reactive Life or a Created Life. In Neuro Linguistic Programming (NLP) it is also referred to as living at cause or at effect. This is a scale of characteristics. You may be more "in effect" in some areas of your life and more "at cause" in others. You may practice some aspects to a greater or lesser degree. These are not personality labels. They are ways of thinking and operating which you will flow in and out of at different periods of your life and in different experiences. I encourage you to use the following as information rather than judgement, and to be open to reflect honestly as to where you are on the scale at a given time.

Characteristics of a Reactive Life/ In Effect

People who place themselves at the effect end of the continuum are essentially saying, "I am not responsible for what I feel or how I act; someone or something else is." They have given their power away, because if other people determine how you feel then they can manipulate you. Being at effect is taking the persona of a victim. It includes characteristics such as:

➤ thinking that things happen in your life because of something someone or something else did

➤ having lots of reasons why you didn't do what you wanted, or get what you wanted

➤ frequently blaming others for your current situation in life.

➤ believing that your emotions are caused by something outside of you, that they are something which just happens to you, or that other people cause them in you e.g. saying/thinking things like: "She made me so angry", or "he upset me", or "this traffic jam is so frustrating".

➤ taking responsibility for people and things that aren't actually your responsibility, which includes anything you have no control over. This could be because you are trying to please everybody, or because you do not feel sufficient self-worth to set appropriate boundaries for what you take on, or because you are living in survival stress mode and simply take on everything because you are not allowing yourself the mental space to decide whether you need to or not

➤ using experiences of the past as the reason for why you are the way you are, or have the limitations you do, or why you haven't achieved what you want in life.

➤ reacting with defence and blame when someone raises an issue with you. For example, if someone tells you they felt hurt by something you said, an 'at effect' response is to think that person made you feel guilty or criticised you so you seek to defend yourself against them and blame them for making you feel uncomfortable.

➢ asking why questions of life such as: "Why is this always happening to me?", "Why are you being mean to me"

➢ thinking that you can only feel happy, satisfied or successful if certain external conditions are met, e.g. thinking "I'll be happy when . . . [this person does this], or "I'll feel successful when . . . [I am acknowledged in this way].

➢ living from a place of unconscious, habitual compulsivity and craving

➢ self-abandoning

➢ Settling for getting the lowest, the least, the last, the dregs and/or less than others and less than you deserve

Characteristics of a Created Life/ At Cause

When you are living a created life, you understand that you can effectively manage your thoughts and feelings and that how you think and feel creates how you perceive and experience life, and therefore creates how life is for you. You take full responsibility for your thoughts, feelings and behaviour. Characteristics of being "at cause" include:

➢ accepting that your current situation is the result of your conscious and unconscious choices and decisions up until this point

➢ taking personal responsibility and owning your thoughts, feelings and actions

➢ believing that you are in charge of how you perceive, experience and respond to all the events of your life

- understanding that your emotions are a chemical response triggered in your body by how you think about what you are experiencing and what meaning you are giving it

- setting healthy boundaries about what you choose to take on, about who you interact with, and about managing your personal space

- having the belief that life happens with you rather than to you

- believing/knowing that your sense of happiness, satisfaction and success comes from your internal thoughts and feelings and how you choose to perceive your life experience

- living from a place of conscious, self-responsible, intentional creation

- self-honouring

- thriving

An Empowered Understanding of Your Thoughts and Feelings

It may feel like external triggers (things people say or do, or life experiences) are causing emotional responses in you because the internal process happens so fast, but living a created life means knowing that in fact,

Between stimulus and response there is a space.
In that space is our power to choose our response

Viktor Frankl: Man's Search for Meaning

And that

Quality of life depends on what happens in
the space between stimulus and response

Steven Covey: The 7 Habits of Highly Effective People

A stimulus could be something someone did, or something someone said, or the tone of voice they said it in, or the expression on their face when they said it. For it to register as a stimulus to you at all, your mind has to interpret it as significant to you in some way. You evaluate the incoming sensory information in light of your existing belief system and past experiences and give it a meaning, which then stimulates an emotional response in you, a feeling. All this happens at an unconscious level, usually in seconds. When you repeatedly respond to the same or a similar stimulus in the same way, then you strengthen the neural pathways that link that stimulus to that response and develop a habitual, automatic pattern of response which can strengthen your belief that your feelings are caused by people and circumstances outside of you, because your emotional response to them is completely reactive and unconscious. To live a created life, you need to consistently bring your conscious awareness to the present moment to interrupt and question any habitual, automatic patterns of thinking and feeling in response to what you are experiencing.

Expanded Thought Feeling Cycle

Repetition leads to the hardwiring of a certain state of being and you see it as who you are and how life is.

Note that the process starts with thought, and you have control over that.

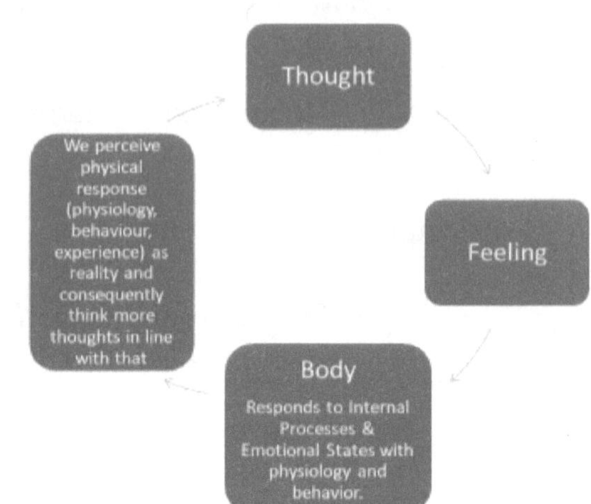

For the most part, your brain is a product of the past. It has been shaped and moulded to become a living record of everything you have learned and experienced up to this point in your life.
To live a created life "at cause" you need to do two key things:

1. Think thoughts that are greater than how you currently feel

2. Interrupt automatic patterns of thought and feeling by being consciously in the present moment

People operating at cause see themselves in an empowered way and can make statements like:
"I am responsible for how I feel and where I am, therefore, I can change that if I want to"

"I can make a difference"

"I can create something new"

"How can I look at this in a more empowered way?"
"What is the opportunity for me in this?"

You can only effectively create positive change in your life when you are operating "at cause".

When you move from thinking life happens to you, to accepting that life happens because of you, you begin to see that life happens for you.

Reactive Life	Created Life
Effect	Cause
Trying	Deciding
Dictated by circumstances and others	Directed by you
Life happens *to* me	Life happens *for* me
Blame	Personal responsibility
Should, need	Want, desire
Obligation	Choice
Frustrated, resentful	Confident, empowered
Reasons	Results

Living "at effect" and living "at cause" are opposite ends of a continuum of behaviour. You may be more towards the "at effect" end most of the time, but in some situations are more towards the "at cause" end of the continuum, or vice versa. The key is to become aware of when you are living in a reactive way, "at effect", and reflect on what is causing you to think and behave in this way:

> What beliefs and habitual patterns of thinking, feeling and doing are you operating from?
> Are they serving you?
> Is there a way of thinking that would serve you more?
> Are you living with a consistent high degree of stress?
> If so, what can you do to reduce the stress?
> How can you love and accept yourself more?

You were born to be a deliberate creator,
not a creator by default.

You were born to offer your vibration deliberately so that you could
have the joyful experience of witnessing the becoming
of your conscious focus.

You did not come to be a creator by default who just waits for things
to show up and then has positive or negative reactions to them.

Abraham Hicks

Give Yourself Permission

Living your created life is all about identifying and living what you love. One of the key reasons that people don't do more of what they love is because they feel selfish or guilty when they do. Most of us have grown up with embedded beliefs like:
- It is better to give than to receive
- Self-lessness is a virtue
- Always put others first
- Don't be selfish

We also frequently hear and repeat statements like:
- This is sinfully delicious
- We're having too much fun

- This is my guilty pleasure
- He's drop-dead gorgeous

For more detailed information about how to shift beliefs that no longer serve you see chapter 4: How to Release Limiting Thoughts and Beliefs, or my *10 Steps to Happiness book*. For now, be open to knowing that the best way to give to others is to give to yourself first. If you are giving to others from a depleted state, then you are giving them half-measures and dregs. You think you are serving them, but really everyone is getting low-level input. Often, we over-give because we lack a strong sense of self-love and self-worth. We put everyone else's needs before our own to keep everybody happy, and to try and earn their acceptance and love. Unfortunately, this doesn't really work. When you give beyond your resources, you are disrespecting yourself, and you are teaching others to treat you with disrespect. Moreover, relationships are most fulfilling when both people interact from a place of inner fulness rather than inner need.

You are not just allowed to feel pleasure, you are biologically wired to feel it.

The human body produces a wide variety of neurotransmitters which make us feel good, and many of those feel-good transmitters are connected to biological healing processes. The main four feel-good neurotransmitters are Serotonin, Dopamine, Endorphins and Nitric Oxide. In my book 10 Steps to Happiness, I dedicate a whole chapter to explaining what these do in your body and how you can naturally and easily increase them. When we feel emotions such as joy, love and gratitude, it stimulates responses in our body that boost our immune system, increase longevity and reduces stress and pain. When you do what you love and experience enjoyment, it radiates throughout your body restoring your physical health and vitality, and the energy of it flows out into the world around you.

What You Love is Your Purpose

Another reason why doing more of what you love is important is because it helps you to live your purpose. Feeling a sense of purpose in life is key to happiness. Many people go searching to find their purpose in something external to themselves. However, I believe that your passion is your purpose.

Your purpose is the thing that lights you up. It is the thing that you could engage in or talk about for hours and still feel energised. It is the thing that you would choose to do if time and money were not an issue. That is what you are wired to do. It is what you are here for.

Your purpose does not have to be big and grand. It does not have to serve greater humanity in some momentous way. Your purpose could be growing beautiful flowers, or making crochet toys, or swimming, or repairing motorcycles. When you engage in your passion and it fills you with radiant energy, that has an incredibly positive impact on both you and the world. Happiness breeds happiness; discontent breeds discontent. The Law of Attraction says that you attract more of the energy you vibrate, and that affects not only you, but everyone around you. When you feel enjoyment, you radiate positive energy, and that in and of itself is giving something wonderful to others.

Create Time

The second key reason people don't do more of what they love is because they perceive that they don't have enough time. When you next think you do not have time to do what you really want to and enjoy, then try this rephrase: instead of saying "I don't have time", say, "This is not important to me", or, "My happiness is not important". That is what you are really saying when you choose to believe that you do not have time to do things you love and which nourish you.

When you do not think and act as if your happiness is important, you also teach those around you to think and act like your happiness is not important, and by default, that their happiness is not important.

Time is actually an unlimited resource – it never stops. There is always more time. How we choose to perceive and use time determines how we experience it in our lives. We can create time to do more of what we love by adopting an empowered mind-set about how we see time. I really like this affirmation from the music track Currentsea by Toni Jones:

Time expands for me

There is power in decision

In the wise words of Yoda from Star Wars, "Do or do not, there is no try." There is a big difference in trying to do something versus deciding to do it. Saying you will try and do something is like saying "maybe" as a parent - there's a possibility of a yes, but it's probably a no. Trying is "at effect", whereas deciding is "at cause". Deciding is a commitment to yourself, based in clarity and self-worth. I invite you to swap the words "I will try" for "I choose" or "I decide".

When you decide that it is important for you to do more of what you love, and decide to give yourself permission to seek your own pleasure, then you create the time to do that, and the rest of your life begins to shape around it. Your routines and habits begin to shift to accommodate what you have decided and focused on doing.

The key is usually choosing to believe that you are allowed to use time for your own enjoyment. A belief is simply a thought that is frequently repeated. We change our beliefs by choosing to consistently shift our focus to what we want to become reality in our lives and by choosing thoughts that serve us and then taking action on them. John Assaraf encourages us to ask, "Is what I am spending my time on worthy of my life?" You are not just trading your time for things; you are also trading your life. What experiences do you want to choose to trade your life for?

Now that you have an understanding of the underlying mindset, the what, let's move on to the how. I have put together a four-step process to help you gain clarity about what you really want, plan each day around your true priorities, and then create the life you desire through focused thought and action.

How to Live a Created Life

Below is my four-step process to focus your thoughts and energy to reduce stress, do less, and receive more:

Step 1: Visualise
Step 2: Harmonise
Step 3: Prioritise
Step 4: Actualise

This process will take about 10-15 minutes in the morning and evening. Think of it as an investment of time, rather than it "taking" time. Planning and reviewing your life in this way will help you to do the things that are most important, and do them efficiently and effectively. It will reduce stress, and keep you from giving your time and energy away to things and people that do not serve you. If 30 minutes a day sounds a lot, you could decide to try it for just a week, start with doing just one part of it, or do it with someone else, which may help it to seem more manageable.

Two Key things to Make this Work:
Safety and Worthiness

Your mind consists of your conscious mind, the part you actively think with, and your subconscious mind, the part that runs all your deeply embedded programmes on auto-pilot. In order to effectively create what you want in life, you need to get both of these aspects of mind on board. Otherwise, your conscious mind is putting out one energy signal, and your subconscious mind is putting out a different one, and your energy is split in two directions and connecting to different things. This is why you can make a decision to work towards a new goal and then feel like all sorts of stuff comes up to sabotage it.

Your subconscious mind is largely focused on keeping you alive and safe. Anything new or unknown is a possible threat, especially if it has things in common with things that have caused you hurt or harm in the past. For example, there is actually no logical reason that just because your past partner cheated on you that your next partner will, but because there are things in common (romantic partner, same gender of person, similar activities engaged in together) your subconscious mind red flags it as unsafe and expects that same thing to happen.

The two most common blocks that reside in your subconscious are patterns of belief around being unsafe and being unworthy. The good news is that you can calm and re-programme your sub-conscious mind. The easiest way to calm your subconscious mind is to use your body to regulate your nervous system. If your body feels relaxed, then your subconscious mind will interpret the situation as safe. When you bring your body into a relaxed state using breathwork, meditation, slow movement or gentle music and then visualise or act on your intentions, then your subconscious mind will be programmed to feel safety with that experience and not put up fearful resistant energy to it.

Worthiness is a decision. Being told that you are unworthy is an opinion, not a truth. Choosing to believe that you are unworthy is a pattern of thought, not a truth. If you can choose a pattern of thought that you are unworthy, then you can shift and choose to embed a new pattern of thought that you are worthy. Both are just ways of perceiving yourself. You do not need to earn or prove your worth on a spiritual level. You are life. You are the energy of the Universe and your body is literally made of star-dust. At your essence you are worthy. All you need to do is decide that this is the opinion, the belief, that you want to hold. Give yourself permission to think that, and let other people's opinions stay with them.

This also connects with giving yourself permission. Quite often what is blocking you or keeping you stuck is you needing to give yourself permission to make a change, to think a different way, to act in a new way, to set boundaries, to ask for what you want and to have what you want. Most of your limits and fears are internal and created by you.

Step 1: Visualise

You get in life what you have the courage to ask for.
- Oprah Winfrey

The first step in creating is having an energised vision. This is a vision with emotion attached to it.

To begin the fulfilled life planning process, set aside 30 minutes to an hour to brainstorm and then clarify your current desires and intentions. This will be a one-off practice, although you may repeat it as your desires become physical reality and you can focus on new ones. Write down any responses you have to the questions below. Think about what you would really like, what you really want and not just what you think you can have, or what is currently possible. Also, make it specific to you and things you have control over. You cannot change how other people feel for example, or make them do what you want them to do. If you want someone or something to change, then think about what that change would mean to you and what it would give you. For example, would you feel more relaxed, or have more freedom, or feel appreciated? These outcomes are your true desire. That is what you really want rather than an action that you think will give you that.

Reflection questions to help you clarify your desires and intentions:

- ➢ What are some key desires you have for yourself right now?
- ➢ If you could change something in your life, what would it be?
- ➢ Why do you want that? What is the feeling or state of being you desire from that?

➤ What gives you bliss? What do you feel uplifted by?

How to set intentions

Look at your answers to the questions above and choose one or two desires to focus on now. Write them in the present tense as if they are already happening and combine what you want to happen and the feeling you desire connected to that e.g. "I am experiencing happiness and success in my teaching work", or "I am enjoying meeting and dating women who are self-aware, kind and fun."

If you find it challenging to state something in the present tense when it is not your current reality, it may help to think of it as planting the seeds of what you want to grow. For example, planting the seed that is "I am feeling grounded and free living in a home I own and love surrounded by nature."

Intentions versus Goals

Goals are often specific and time-bound. While this can create focus, it can also create rigidity of thinking, over-doing, and feelings of anxiety, failure and disappointment. People who are very goal oriented may achieve a lot, but often at the expense of their own health and well-being and their relationships with others, because all that matters to them is the finish line. Setting a time to achieve something by can create motivation, and it can also create feelings of anxiety about reaching your goal in time, and stress shuts down the creative thinking parts of the brain. If you don't achieve your goal by the due date, then it can stimulate feelings of failure, embarrassment and disappointment, and decreased motivation to set any further goals.

It is not the "what" that is most important, it is the "why". It is not some achievement or thing you want, but how you think having that will make you feel. What you actually want is to feel states of being such as satisfaction, love, and joy. In essence what we are always reaching for is ways to feel good. Goals focus you on a specific what, which is only one pathway for you to attain the state and feeling you want. Setting intentions in the way outlined in this book focuses you on the why, and creates openness for you to experience that in all sorts of ways that you may not have thought of.

Goal setting:
- keeps you focused on a future end achievement
- makes you very aware of the gap between where you are and what you desire
- often comes from a place that something is "wrong" and you need to fix it
- often leads to feelings of anxiety in terms of achieving what you want
- focuses on effort, striving and making things happen
- ego based

With intentions, the journey is part of living the intention. It is a process of development. You are not chasing something "out there", you are embodying more and more of what you want on a day-to-day basis. Intention setting is grounded in purpose and focus. It is about living purposefully rather than striving for achievements.

Intention setting:
- focuses on who you are being rather than what you are doing
- development rather than achievement
- brings you to the present and how you can live what you want now
- soul based

Our greatest accomplishments often arise unexpectedly, sometimes with results that surpass our aspirations, when we remain in the process, that is, flexible and allowing for the new to form or appear.

*Being in process in this way is the mine of our richest treasures
and the source of our greatness.*

Anat Baniel – Move into Life

Live Your Bliss Daily

Focus in on what you wrote for things that give you bliss and things that uplift you. Rank your answers in order from most blissful/uplifting in decreasing order. These are the things that most effectively nourish you. Make it a priority to do more of the things that are pleasing to you. On the Daily Focus Sheet, which I explain in the Prioritize section of this book, there is a space to write down the top three things that give you bliss, to prompt you to plan engaging with aspects of these every day.

How to Visualise Effectively

*The power of your mind is the only power that matters, and all the other stuff you do is just for the pleasure of enhancing what you've really done with your mind.
All the real power is the focus [of your mind].*

Abraham Hicks

As Dr Joe Dispenza teaches, combining a clear intention of your future with an elevated emotion changes your energy, your brain chemistry, the way your brain works, your genetic expression and stimulates you to evolve. When you think about an experience enough times in your mind, your brain will develop new neural pathways and change to look like the experience has already occurred. Your body also begins to signal your genes in new ways which begins to change your body to look as if the event has already occurred. Your body as the unconscious mind believes it is already living in that future reality in the present moment.

*As you begin to think about a new possibility, and your brain begins
to fire in new patterns, new sequences and new combinations, and you
begin to plan your behaviours, and you begin to review in your mind
and mentally rehearse who you're going to be in your life,
the mere action of mental rehearsal begins to install the
neurological circuits in your brain.*
- Dr Joe Dispenza

The following visioning process is to help clarify and raise your energy to make you more attractive and aligned to all that you want. When you imagine something vividly your subconscious mind responds to it in the same way as a real physical experience. This means that it is a great way to teach your nervous system and body what it would be like to have that experience, and also that it is safe and possible for you to have that experience. Your subconscious mind's primary focus is to keep you safe, which means that it likes things that are familiar and routine and is resistant to change. Visualisation is an easy way to help your subconscious mind to accept change and for your neural networks to rewire to form an identity of yourself as a person who has or does the thing that you are imagining. Often to step into something new, we have to grow and adapt into a new identity. We can do that through physical experience, and we can speed up the process through engaging in visualisation.

You can engage in visualisation at any time that works for you, however the best times to visualise are in the evening just before you go to sleep, and in the morning when you first wake up. As you drift into sleep your subconscious mind becomes more receptive, making it a very effective time to plant your intentions and desires in your mind and body by imagining and feeling what it could be like to have what you want. This sets your subconscious mind to work on your goals and desires while you sleep. When you first wake up in the morning you are also very receptive, and your energy is usually settled and clear. Visualising a positive intention for what you desire at this point sets your energy and focus well for the day to come. It helps you start your day from a place of appreciation, excitement, fun, love and personal power and truth. Once you get familiar with the process, the other time you can use during the day is whenever you are waiting, for example waiting in line at the supermarket, or waiting for a meal order to be ready. Also, any time that you would normally turn to scrolling on your phone, or watching un-enriching things on television could be used to constructively visualise instead. This might seem radical, but if you want your life to radically change, then you need to do things in a radically different way.

A Step-by-Step Process for Effective Visualisation

Step 1: Get into a relaxed, present state to create a sense of safety in your body
Create a regular meditation place at home. Somewhere comfortable and quiet where you won't be disturbed. I recommend sitting in a chair to do visualisation as you are less likely to fall asleep during the practice and it keeps your bed as your place for sleep.

One of the easiest ways to move into a relaxed present state is to bring your focus to your breath for about 5 minutes, and to engage in belly/diaphragmatic breathing. Breathe in through your nose into the abdomen. Feel the air come in through your nose and throat and feel your diaphragm move down, your belly rise, and your ribcage expand out to the sides. It may feel like your lower ribcage is opening out as you breathe in and relaxing back to neutral when you breathe out. For the exhale let your breath flow out naturally and feel your abdomen relax down and the air come out through your nose or mouth. Let your exhale be slightly longer than your inhale. Focusing on your breath coming in and out of your body and the sensations in your body brings your awareness into the present moment. Diaphragmatic breathing also:
- lowers heart rate and blood pressure
- decreases muscle tension

- increases blood oxygenation
- brings warmth to the hands and feet
- increases energy and motivation
- improves concentration
- reduces stress hormones
- activates the body's relaxation response

These conditions in your physical body signal to your subconscious mind that you are safe and all is well, which opens it to receive new information and experiences.

Step 2: Use gratitude and appreciation to raise your emotional frequency

You can fill in the "End of Day Review" section on the Daily Focus Sheet to do this, or write in a gratitude journal, or sit and think of things that you are thankful for, or that you like or love (appreciation). Let your heart open and expand with a feeling of love and gratitude, and deeply feel all the good feelings as sensations in your body. American Psychologist and author Dr Rick Hansen calls this "taking in the good."

You may also like to use somatic touch or tapping to deepen your body's ability to move out of stress and into a relaxed and receiving state. Some ways you can do this are:

- tap your fingertips just under your collarbone around the centre of your chest with one or both hands
- tap the crown at the very top of your head with your fingertips
- place one hand on your heart energy centre in the middle of your chest, or one hand on your heart and the other on your belly

Raising the emotional frequency that you are feeling connects you to, and draws to you, good things that also have a high vibrational frequency of love, peace, appreciation and joy. It also connects your desire with these good feelings so that whenever you feel them, you are also tuning into and attracting your desire.

Step 3: Imagine your desire in full sensory detail
Bring to mind your current core desire, what you want to create in your life, or a positive focus statement (see Appendix one of this book for suggestions) connected to your core desire. Imagine having this now and imagine how it would look and feel to flow with the feelings you want to feel, to be the person you want to be, and to speak, move and act as if you are already living your desire. In this moment let go of it needing to be rational or logical and simply tune in to your full heart's desire.

Write a story in your head or physically write it, or create it like a movie in your mind. See or sense it as if through your own eyes, in first person. Bring in all your senses. What do you see? What do you hear? What do you smell? What are you touching or feeling with your hands or body? What do you taste? You could bring to mind one of the tasks or activities that you are going to do today. Feel how you want to feel while you are doing it. See yourself taking actions that achieve the result you want. Play with this, see it as fun and creative.

Focus on creating how you will experience this, and what you would like to do, rather than what other people will think and feel. You may find that the vision starts to unfold unconsciously/intuitively in your mind as if it is being received from somewhere else and it may feel spiritually guided. If a negative thought like "that can't happen" or "I can't do that" comes up, or a feeling of fear or doubt or resistance, then just acknowledge it. Notice it as information about the programmes stored in your subconscious mind that you can reframe and re-programme. Then find a way to let it flow through. Sometimes we just need to release these thoughts and feelings by imagining them flowing away from us on a river, or floating away like a cloud in the sky. You can also release the energy of feelings by sighing, or letting out a strong exhale, or giving them sound or movement with your body.

One of the most common sticking points for visualising and using focus statements is the part of our brain that resists them because they are not true. What we actually mean by this is that they are not true according to the current physical reality we are experiencing. What if we opened the definition of what truth is? These things are true as thoughts that we have created. They are true in the sense that they are our true desires. They are true as seeds of change that we are planting. The elevation of science has created the idea that there is such a thing as objective truth, but really there is no such thing. Everything is perception and everything is in a constant state of movement and change. Even if everyone was looking at the same physical table, they would perceive it differently due to differences in viewpoint and sensory function, and they would describe it with different language which has different nuances of meaning. The truth of your reality actually only exists in the way you perceive and describe it. You can use that to make a conscious choice to perceive and describe reality in a way that feels good to you.

Step 4: Allow time to integrate and receive
At the end of the visualisation process sit for a few minutes in silence to let what you have experienced be fully integrated into your mind and body.

Roadblocks That You May Experience

Resistant Emotions

When resistant emotions arise such as fear, frustration, sadness, hurt, or disappointment, then take a pause to acknowledge them, feel them, and notice any sensations in your body as you feel them. Accept any feelings with compassion. They are a part of you being expressed. You can use your breath or body movement or vocalisation to express and release the energy of any emotion and let it be fully felt. When you do this, most emotions will move through you quickly as energy. If they do not, then they may be attached to deep subconscious woundings, and you may wish to get support from a professional trained in somatic or embodiment work such as myself.

Being too Specific about What you are Asking For
When you become attached to your desire being manifested in a specific way then it can create resistance. The more specific you are, the tighter your focus, and the more attachment you have to a specific outcome. This can lead to inflexible thinking, and feelings of disappointment, frustration, sadness and despair when things don't happen in the way you think they should.

Focus on what you want to feel, trust that good things flow to you and leave room for the magic of the universe to bring components together in a way that is more satisfying than you could imagine from your limited physical perspective. It is the energy that is the key thing, not the specifics of the vision. Be playful with the process, enjoy the visioning process itself and the feelings in the moment. Let go of any attachment to the outcome. It can help to say at the end of your visioning, "I would like this or something better." Come to visioning with the intention of allowing rather than asking for something or making something happen. Visioning is not constantly asking the Universe for something, The Universe knows all of what you want – you don't need to keep telling it. Visioning is to allow your conscious and unconscious mind and body to move into the frequency of what you want.

If you find it hard to visualise a strong desire without a sense of sadness or frustration at not having it yet, then use a different desire for this process, one that you don't have as much attachment to. A desire that that you can just play with in the energy of "wouldn't it be nice", as in, "I'd like this but I'm not overly invested in it." Or, use a more general focus statement connected to the theme of your desire, such as a soul truth from Appendix one of this book. This can help you create a higher-level feeling energy that is more attractive to other things that give you high level feeling energy. It can be an easier pathway.

Confusion
Confusion is the opposite of clarity. Confusion about knowing what you want or where to begin usually stems from a habitual pattern of living a reactive life on autopilot and responding to whatever life is demanding of you, or from feeling fearful or unsafe to make decisions for yourself. Alternatively, you may get stuck with thinking that you have to choose the right core desire to get started.

If you have been living on autopilot, "at effect", and have never really stopped to think about what you really want, then the first thing to do is give yourself space and permission to start asking that question and reflecting on the answer: "What do I really want?" It may take some time (days, weeks, months) to begin to get some clarity about what you truly want. Thinking about what you loved when you were a child may help, or reading through the focus statements in the appendix of this book and noticing which ones feel really good to you.

If you feel fearful or unsafe to make decisions for yourself then you may need to do some personal development work to release beliefs and emotional energy creating that limitation for you. Alternatively, you may need to give yourself permission to start anywhere and to know that you can't fail. This connects into the third reason above for why you may feel confusion: perfectionism. You can't get this wrong. Any desire that you start with is fine, and it is okay if you need to adjust or change it later. This planning process is designed to help you get to know yourself better and better and to evolve. Wherever you start, wherever you are at, is the right place to begin. Nothing needs to be in place or sorted or right. You can start in the middle of a mess. This process will hopefully help you to work your way out of that, unless you learn that you actually like the mess. The only necessary thing is to show up and keep showing up, because this only works if you do it.

Complacency
Complacency is the opposite of burning desire (and decision). It can come in two main forms: settling and playing small.

Settling is: "this is good enough"
Playing small is: "I don't want to be greedy or too much"

Underlying both of these can be doubt about your ability or your worthiness, for example thoughts such as: I'm too old . . . too young . . . don't have the right skills . . . it is wrong to ask for too much . . . it isn't safe to stand out . . etc.

All of these are only beliefs, merely one pattern of thought. You need to decide if they are true for you or not, and if they are not, then choose a new more empowering thought to think habitually. The focus statements in the appendix of this book may be helpful for that.

Settling can also be a sign that your core desire is not big enough or emotionally engaging enough for you, in other words, you don't want it enough. You need to key into a core desire that is crystal clear and emotionally engaging enough for you that it inspires you to do what you really want to do. Sometimes, the first foundational motivation for you can be a strong decision that you are able to have more in your life, that you have had enough of settling or just getting by, and/or that you are worthy to have more.

Motivation comes in two forms and there is a difference between motivation and inspiration. Some people are more motivated by what they want to avoid and some people are more motivated by what they want to gain. Identify some clear key motivating points for you, either pain points (I want to do this because I really don't want that), or pleasure points (I want to do this because I really want that). Motivation involves a sense of effort and is usually based in a sense of lack, fear or external expectations or priorities. We need motivation when we are doing things to look good to others or achieve something that society values. Inspiration is internal. Inspired action comes from connecting with your authentic self and your true personal desires and feels effortless. Inspiration gives you energy. Set the intention of taking inspired action rather than motivated action and consistently reflect on what beliefs or patterns of thought/behaviour may underlie any resistance you feel, why you are doing something, and what is most important to you.

Distraction
This is a big one because you will experience distraction in many forms. Social media and television will distract you. Your friends and family will distract you with their needs, priorities and problems. Work will distract you. Lack of money will distract you. Know that you will get distracted and make a plan for how to deal with it. Using the Daily Focus Sheet will help you stay focused and manage distractions, especially those based around things you have to do and things you should do i.e. things other people want you to do. Sometimes though, it just comes down to whether you choose to watch another television episode before you go to bed, or turn the TV off and sit and reflect on your day and visualise your desires. In cases like that, the solution can be the same as for complacency. To overcome the draw of that distraction, your desire needs to be more compelling than the distraction. You need to be clear about what each of those choices will bring you, and what you really want.

On a practical level, it can be helpful to set reminders or create cues in your routine that prompt you. One of the best ways to create a new habit is to connect the new activity to an activity that you already do habitually. For example, I fill in my daily focus sheet while I have my breakfast each morning.

Unsupportive External Environment
Your friends, family and work colleagues may not understand what you are trying to do. They may ridicule you, or try and put their doubts and fears on you. It is safest to only share what you are doing with other people who you know are in agreement and understanding with these processes, and people who are going to celebrate with you and encourage you. For everyone else, let your life speak rather than your words. Just let people notice the positive changes in you and your life and then if they ask questions, you can share a little about the processes you have been using.

Not Seeing Physical Results
Understand that this is a practice. Things only work when you do them, and in this case, they work when you do them consistently and repeatedly. One effective way to create a new habit is to connect it to something you already routinely do. For example, doing your visioning at a regular time as part of a regular routine signals to your mind that it is time to wind down and move into a relaxed, open receiving state.

There will be days when you get distracted or another responsibility comes up and you miss doing your practice for that day. It's okay. Success is not getting it right 100% of the time. Success is constantly coming back to your intention and practice as and when you can. Keep showing up and doing the practices and change will happen. Sometimes it may happen quickly or in big ways, and other times the shift will be gradual and subtle. Keep focused on your intention and the Universe will meet you. Sometimes that may not look like what you thought it would. Sometimes the quickest and easiest path to you evolving is by experiencing something unwanted and/or uncomfortable that makes you ask for something new, or ask for what you want more clearly, or more strongly, or learn something and grow in a way that you need to in order to get where you want to go.

Creation is a process. Seeds take time to germinate, babies go through a gestation process. Look for ways that you are feeling the feelings that you desire more than looking for physical things or experiences coming into your life. Energy also has momentum. For example, if you have been operating with a lot of fearful thoughts and feelings for an extended period, then there has been a big momentum build up over time and you can't instantly shift that. It will take time to shift the energy momentum from one direction to another. It is like trying to turn a corner in a speeding car, you have to slow the car down first and then you can begin turning the corner. The first and most important step is simply to become aware of where you already have momentum that you would like to shift. What things are you doing that are not serving you? What are you giving your attention to that is making you feel anxious or not enough? Then what is the flip side of that? If that is what you don't want, then what do you want? Once you have clarity about that, then put your focus on what you desire.

This is a lifelong journey because life is constantly changing and expanding. What I am sharing with you in this book are tools to support you to live your best life. You will get better and better at using them with practice, and get greater and greater results. However, a great life is one that is lived fully and that means constant growth and expansion. Learn to enjoy the journey of it all, the experience of it ALL. Every moment lived is a gift of experience and an opportunity for more.

Letting Go and Moving On
Sometimes, choosing something new, something more, means letting go of something you already have. For example, it might call you to leave your current job for a new one, or it might call you to transition from a relationship that is limiting you, or no

longer a good fit for you. Life is constantly changing anyway. Things and people will come and go in your life whether you choose for them to or not. Getting clear about what you really want and what does and doesn't serve your highest good does sometimes accelerate that though. One of the most empowering skills you can learn is how to make what author Geri Reid Suster calls "Graceful Exits". Making graceful exits in your life involves being able to appreciate what you had without attachment to it; to celebrate all that experience was, and to understand the power and growth that comes from moving on while holding yourself with compassion and authenticity.

Release Limiting Thoughts and Beliefs

Limiting thoughts and beliefs are another roadblock, but this is a big one that everyone will encounter so I have dedicated a whole chapter to it. It is common and normal to have fearful and limiting thoughts and feelings when you step into taking full responsibility for your life and creating something new. These may be:

- fear of failure
- fear of success
- fear of abandonment by friends/family if you become successful
- fear of losing the good you have if you take the risk of having more
- feeling like a fraud to step out and do what you want to do
- fear of not being enough e.g. too old, too young, not qualified enough, to big, too small etc.
- fear of being judged as unspiritual if you desire money or material things

Fearful and limiting thoughts and feelings are not truths, they are purely thoughts and feelings, and are usually based on things you have been taught or experienced in the past. They are connected to old subconscious programming. Celebrate when they come up because it means the unconscious has become conscious, and awareness of them gives you choice. They are not a sign that anything is going wrong. They are simply an element of being human.

What we think, determines what we do, and shapes how our life is for us. To change our life, we need to change our thoughts. Easier said than done, right? How do we stop thinking or believing something? What about sub-conscious thoughts that operate without us even being aware of them?

In this chapter I will give you an easy three-part process to rewrite and release limiting beliefs, however, first, there are two prefaces that you need to accept:

1. Beliefs are simply thoughts you have been repeatedly exposed to. They are not necessarily true, and it is okay to change what you believe.
Do you still believe everything you believed as a child? Of course you don't. We learn and grow and our thoughts and beliefs can change as we do.

2. You are allowed to choose what you want to believe.

This is often the concept many people get stuck with: accepting that they are ALLOWED to choose what they believe. We often feel that what we believe has to be true in some objective sense, or feel fearful about choosing to think something quite different from what most other people think. Coming to a place where you allow yourself to choose thoughts and beliefs that serve you is an empowering process based in learning to accept and know your inherent worth. However, if you are only at the beginning of your journey to step into your role as creator in your life, these three elements will still help you to make significant shifts in the way you think.

Part 1. Awareness

This step is about developing an awareness that you have a pattern of thinking that you would like to change i.e. becoming conscious of what you are thinking and the beliefs you are operating from. Many people operate on auto-pilot. They do not take time to reflect on what they are thinking, or to question their thinking or beliefs. They prefer to avoid uncomfortable thoughts and feelings through distractions such as alcohol, media, work, excessive effort, and drugs.

You do not need to bring up and rehash old experiences and hurts in order to understand why you think and feel the way you do. You can simply start from where you are at now. Accept that for whatever reason, you currently have a certain pattern of thinking or belief. Awareness is acknowledging that belief, and then beginning to question whether it serves you.

Many people worry about subconscious beliefs, and whether they are lurking under the surface sabotaging our efforts to live a positive, expansive life. If a belief does not carry enough emotional charge (energy) for you to become aware of it operating in your life, then it will not have enough energy to have any significant impact. If you learn to become conscious and aware of the thoughts that are active in your mind, then you will be able to address all the beliefs that are influencing your life.

Personally, I find that awareness occurs in an upward spiral. By this I mean that when you become aware of a deep belief or pattern of thinking that is operating and manage it on one level, as you move through life you will probably encounter it again but from a different perspective and higher level of awareness. Evolution is a process. Remember, just because a limiting belief may take a while to shift does not mean that growth is not happening. Hold yourself with love and compassion and keep moving forward.

Six Ways to Become Aware of What You Believe

1. Stream of consciousness journaling

Pick a topic that has a strong emotional charge such as money, love, work, life is hard, worthiness or happiness, and then write whatever comes to you about that topic in a journal, or type it into a document. Don't worry about neatness, spelling or grammar. Simply write whatever flows. You can also record your ideas as images or a mind-map. Once you are finished, look at what you recorded in your journal, and you will be able to identify some key thoughts and beliefs.

2. Listen to what you say in conversation

Often what we say in the flow of conversation will reveal what we truly think. This seems to be especially the case when we are having a conversation with someone we are not emotionally invested in, such as someone we are sitting beside on a bus, or meet while on holiday

3. Listen to what you say to your children

What are some common statements you make to your children? For example, "You can't have everything you want", "Money doesn't grow on trees", "We don't have enough money for that", "Life isn't fair" etc.

4. Notice when you say, "I can't"

When you say you can't do something or have something, the reason why is probably a limiting belief of some sort. For example, "I can't go on holiday because I don't have enough money". The limiting belief is, "I don't have enough money".

Sometimes we need to dig a little deeper underneath our reason. For example, a woman might think, "I can't tell my partner how I truly feel because it might hurt him." Why might this woman feel like she is not allowed to be honest because of how the other person would respond? It could be the belief: "I need to keep the peace in relationships", or "a good relationship involves compromise", or "it is wrong to hurt others", or "a good person puts the needs of others before their own", or "If I am honest, I will be rejected". You can uncover your deeper reasons for why you think you can't do something by continuously asking the question, "How come?". For example, if you think, "I can't ask that person on a date because they'd probably say no", then you can ask yourself, "How come I think they'll say no?". This will help to uncover deeper beliefs, which in this case may be thoughts like, "I am not attractive enough", or "People won't think I can have a successful relationship because I have had failed relationships in the past" i.e. "I am a failure at relationships".

5. Notice what and who you judge

When you judge someone or something, it is all about you, not them. Your judgements come from your values and beliefs in response to something that triggers you. For example, I became aware that I was feeling judgement and resistance towards an incredibly beautiful woman who has become very successful teaching manifestation tools. My judgement was that she was probably so successful because she is very physically attractive and sexy. When I became conscious of that judgement and sat with it, I became aware that one of my limiting beliefs was that I am not attractive enough to be successful. On the surface, judgements and resistance seem to indicate that we don't like something, but when you look deeper, they often point to things that we want, but don't think we can have, or don't feel safe to have.

6. Think of a problem or situation in your life that you are struggling with or where you feel stuck, and write a story about it as if it were happening to someone else.

Think of why the character in the story might be having this issue, or why they feel like they can't take certain options. What beliefs might this character be under the influence of? Doing this helps us to see the problem from a broader perspective, and reduces the emotional charge and stress, which frees up our creative thinking.

Once you have become aware of a belief you can challenge it and decide if you want to keep it. Remember: A belief is simply a thought that you have been repeatedly exposed to. It is not necessarily true, even if many others believe it. Accept that you are the creator of your life and you have the power and permission to choose thoughts that serve you – that make you feel good.

Let's work through an example:
Common belief: I have to earn my way in life
Let's begin to question this: How come I have to earn my way in life? Who says I have to earn my way in life? Asking 'what if?' questions can help to open your mind to consider other ways of thinking, for example, "What if it was okay for things to come easily to me in life?" Sometimes when we begin reflecting on one pattern of thought or belief, we find there is another underneath it. In this case there are usually underlying beliefs such as: It's not fair to get things when you haven't earned them – life should be fair. However, don't get too stuck in this process. Identifying one to three beliefs at a time is enough. The main aim is simply to become aware of the belief and examine it from the basis of questions such as:
- ➢ Does this belief serve me?
- ➢ How does this limit protect me?
- ➢ Does this thought make me feel good?
- ➢ Do I need to continue to believe this?
- ➢ Is this a thought I would like to shift?
- ➢ How can I rewrite this belief into one that works for me now?

Let go of trying to work out where that belief came from or why you think that way. It is what it is at this point in time. Start from where you are at now and move forward. What we focus on we activate, so only give your attention to limiting, uncomfortable thoughts long enough to realize that you want to create a new pattern of thinking – and then move on to step 2.

Turn the other cheek . . . You've seen this, now look over there.
Abraham Hicks

Part 2. Focus on What You Want

Wherever focus goes, energy flows

Tony Robbins

You don't need to consciously eradicate old thoughts, simply focus on new ones that you would like to think. Energy flows to what you think about. What you focus on grows. If you mentally try to let go of thoughts and beliefs you no longer want to hold onto, then that process of trying to get rid of them sets your focus on them, which continues to activate them for you. Turn your attention to what you want to think and believe. You do not need to fix the old, just create something new.

Be conscious of what you are reading and watching, and conversations you are choosing to take part in. What beliefs are they reinforcing? Feed yourself on things that support how you want to think, who you want to be and what you want your life to be like. If you don't give them attention or fuel of any kind, then your old patterns of thinking will eventually die off on their own. If they pop up from time to time, you can see them as something you used to believe, but now you choose to believe something else. Research has shown that our brains have a self-cleaning mechanism. When you have a new experience, learn something or have a focused thought, it creates new neural pathways in your brain. Neural pathways that get used repeatedly become strengthened. Conversely, synaptic connections that we use less, i.e. thoughts we think or information we retrieve infrequently or not at all, get marked for pruning (deleting) by our microglial cells.

The exception to this appears to be memories that have a very strong emotional charge or thoughts to which we make some sort of strong connection. These are often retained and not pruned. Many of our limiting beliefs are connected to and stem from emotional experiences we have had in the past. When a limiting belief is connected to a strong emotional memory you usually need to first release the emotional charge on the memory in order to be able to shift the attached sub-conscious/unconscious beliefs. There are a number of practices you can use to do this including hypnosis, NLP parts integration technique, somatic therapy, inner child work and energy therapies such as Reiki. I also find I can do it personally through meditation and visualization.

Go easy with it. Focus on consistent subtle shifts. What we resist, persists which means that trying to force change normally doesn't work. Sometimes you may identify a belief that is too emotionally charged or hard for you to look at currently. If that happens know that having an awareness of it is enough to start with, and you can come back to that belief when you feel ready. Merely bringing it into clear awareness is often enough to start it shifting on its own. Choosing to be in acceptance of wherever you are at now, and loving yourself for whatever you are currently feeling creates space for growth to naturally occur. Focus on thinking whatever thoughts feel better for you.

Personally, I am cautious about the practice of repeating affirmations over and over verbally or in your head. If you feel like you need to repeat an affirmation to start to believe it then it is likely that you currently don't believe it, and therefore when you repeat it, you will have some resistance to it. This resistance might be a voice inside going, "You don't really believe that", "That isn't true", and/or "No you're not". If you are thinking something that you feel resistance or negative emotion about, then you will remain stuck in what you don't want. If what you are doing to change a belief feels like hard work, then you need to change your focus because you will be in low frequency energy and not lining up with the high frequency feelings of love, joy and peace that you want.

Find a way to activate a new thought that feels good. Think of it as a pathway to journey on rather than a goal to reach. Use playful language to bypass resistance. Helpful statement starters can be:
"What if . . ."
"I would like to believe . . ."
"I feel good thinking that . . ."

Soft gentle desire is the most powerful desire in the world.
Soft gentle focus on things you want is the most powerful state of
being, because you want it and you allow it.

Abraham Hicks

You don't even need to stay on topic. Reach for any thought that feels better. It could be about anything, not necessarily the belief you are wanting to adopt. Just do more of what makes you feel better, whatever that is. Simply focus on thoughts that make you feel good, whatever they may be. Consistently turn your focus to what you like, to what is going well, to what you have got done, to what you do have, and to what you would like more of. Have fun playing the role of creator in your life.

Part 3. Use Your Body to Shift Energy

You can use your body to help shift stuck patterns of feeling and thought. Here are three ways you can do this:

1. Adopt the body language of the thought or feeling you want
For example: if you want to embed the thought "I am worthy", focus on sitting, standing and walking with your head up, spine extended up, and shoulders back.

This is like doing affirmations with your body. In the example above it is like saying: 'I am worthy" with your body. However, while repeating affirmations verbally or in your head can create resistance, changing your body posture usually bypasses this.

2. Change Your Routine Actions
Any change to the routine actions you do on a regular basis can stimulate a shift in your mental perspective. Things like brushing your teeth with the opposite hand to the one you normally use, or walking a different route to work, or changing the order of the steps you go through to get ready in the morning, take you off auto-pilot and raise your level of awareness. Moreover, new and particularly new complex experiences that involve all of your body and senses, can stimulate the growth of new neurons, and synaptic connections in the hippocampus area of your brain. This is the area of the brain largely responsible for memory and emotional management. Examples of complex physical experiences are learning a new physical skill, walking or cycling over uneven ground, or playing a game of tennis. Essentially any activity where you are constantly having to adjust your body to respond to changing stimulus.

3. Engage regularly in an energy movement practice
Examples of energy movement practices include yoga, Qigong, Tai Chi, Ecstatic dance, Nia and somatic movement. Practices such as these calm your nervous system, and bring your focus to the present moment. Their constant flowing motion demonstrates symbolically that nothing is permanent and change is possible.

Moving your body with flow to music can release energy and emotions in your body without you even necessarily being aware of it. After I had danced my way through the Nia white belt training, I felt like I had physically released a lot of negative thoughts and emotions without having to be conscious of what they were, or apply any kind of mental focus to the process. It simply happened as I moved and danced in the way I felt my body wanted to. This made the process of letting go easy and pleasurable. Afterwards I felt lighter, freer and more confident to show up fully as myself.

Changing your routine actions and engaging in a focused movement practice like yoga, Tai chi or somatic dance brings you mindfully into the present moment. This interrupts habitual unconscious thought patterns, including unconscious limiting beliefs, and creates an easeful opportunity for new positive feelings and thoughts to be embedded.

We cannot be in the present moment and
run our story lines at the same time.

Pema Chodron

Dr Bruce Lipton referred to this process when talking to Dina Proctor about her self-healing practice: "In your case, with your three-minute, three-times-per-day healing meditations, you broke the norm. Those healing meditations constantly and consistently interrupted the tapes that the subconscious was playing. . . Without knowing it, you were doing one of the most powerful things you could have done in your own healing. You stopped listening to the subconscious tapes and started living in the present moment, in effect bringing yourself to your healing."

Consciously being aware of the sensations in your body in order to release stress and tension, including that connected to emotional trauma, is known as somatic therapy (the word somatic is derived from the Greek word "soma" which means living body). Current findings in neuroscience give supporting evidence to somatic psychology practices based on the way the mind influences the body and the body influences the mind. Whenever you become aware that you are thinking limiting, anxious or judgemental thoughts then I invite you to also notice what sensations you feel in your body as you think about them. Sense into what you are feeling and where you are feeling it and imagine opening space around the sensation to let it fully express itself if that feels okay for you. Just observe it and let it be fully felt. You don't need to understand it or give it any meaning. Allowing your body to express in this way can release any emotional energy attached to a thought or belief without having to go into any story about where it came from. I use this process a lot in my group work and one to one coaching.

I don't believe that life has to be hard, and I believe that the source energy of the universe supports each one of us as creators of our lives. You can move forward into who you want to be and the life you want to live with ease and lightness. You can have fun with it. Simply begin where you are at now, and become aware of, and acknowledge, what you would like to be different – to be more than what it currently is. Then, focus on what you like, and use your body to shift energy in an easy, and even pleasurable, way.

Step 2. Harmonize - Listen to Your Heart

The life you want is what you love so it is at the frequency of love

Mary Morrisey - life coach
Founder of the Brave Thinking Institute

Do what you love and what you love will come to you

This step is about connecting into what brings YOU joy, passion and meaning. It is about first connecting into your own wants, intuition and creativity before you consider what other people need or are asking of you. This feeds you emotionally and helps you to create a secure foundation within yourself from which to operate.

I have designed a daily focus sheet to guide you in how to do this. Before you begin filling it in, take a few minutes to sit quietly and do some diaphragmatic breathing which I give instructions for in the previous section on how to visualise effectively. This will awaken your body's energy, and connect you in to the present moment, your body's wisdom and your emotions. Once you have done this, reflect on the following questions. You can use the Daily Focus Sheet for this from Appendix 2 at the back of this book, or your own journal or put them into a digital format.

Question 1: How do I want to feel today?

Instead of focusing on what you want to do or achieve, focus on what you want to FEEL. You can choose a feeling that connects into your core desire which you identified as part of the initial visualising process described in the previous section. Or, you can choose a feeling that relates specifically to what you are going to be doing today. How do you ultimately want to feel as you move through your day? For example, I may decide I want to focus on feeling grounded and balanced if I am going to be doing a lot of computer work which tends to make me feel wired and tired and in my head.

Some Feelings Inspiration

Connected	Happy	Purposeful
Secure	Appreciated	Focused
Belonging	Open	Coherent
Loved	Allowing	Rich
Dynamic	Masterful	Abundant
Calm	Light	Flourishing
Content	Sexy	Thriving
Balanced	Joyful	Well
Peaceful	Creative	Healthy
Confident	Inspired	Relaxed
Blessed	Magnetic	Delighted
Satisfied	Playful	Beautiful
Fulfilled	Supported	Delicious

When you focus on the feeling you want, the why, rather than a specific thing that you think will give you that feeling, you leave space for the magic of the Universe to fulfil your desires in a more wonderful way than you could even imagine. It also enables you to focus on how you can create those feelings in yourself NOW. We attract more of what we are vibrating. If you vibrate the feeling that you want now, it will attract into your life more of what creates that feeling in you. Prioritising what you want to feel is more effective for creating a fulfilling life than prioritising what you want to do or have. Action is still important, but action inspired by your feeling desire. If that sounds a bit too spiritual for you, there is also science behind this.

Is the Law of Attraction Real?

Have you ever noticed that when you feel happy or fall in love then things in your life seem to flow almost magically and everything seems good? Have you also noticed that, conversely, when you feel stressed and worried, everything seems to go wrong, and it can seem like the universe is against you?
This is a common experience, and the science of psychology acknowledges the principle of attraction as an evidence-based phenomenon. There is general consensus that it does occur, but there are various theories for why it happens. Spiritual teachers such as Abraham Hicks and those featured in The Secret call it the universal Law of Attraction. Quantum physics can explain the experience in terms of the connection of similar frequencies, and neuroscience can explain it as the operation of our reticular activating system.

The Principle of Attraction
The principle of attraction, that like attracts like, is an evidence-based phenomenon acknowledged by social science and positive psychology. Research has shown that positivity is associated with better relationships, increased success, more care for the well-being of others, better jobs, improved health, and personality traits and behaviours that help us to be more successful and meet people who can have a positive influence in our lives. Evidence shows that the principle of attraction is part of human experience, but there are various theories as to WHY it occurs.

Do Humans Tune into Frequencies Like a Radio Does?
Let's look at the frequency theory of quantum physics first. One of the concepts of quantum physics is that everything is energy, and that all energy vibrates at a particular frequency.

All vibrations transport their energy by waves. Two of the vibrational waves our brains and bodies emit are thought and emotional waves. These generate electromagnetic energy fields that extend beyond your physical body. Waves have their own vibrational frequency, and each category of waves has a frequency spectrum. One wave category most people are familiar with is light. At the top of the visible light spectrum is violet which has the highest frequency, and at the bottom is red which has the lowest frequency. Another is radio waves. Radio stations are transmitted on one particular sine wave frequency. In order to pick up that station on your radio, it needs to be tuned to that particular frequency and resonating with it. In the same way, energy frequencies resonate with (connect with) other frequencies that are on the same frequency spectrum level.

If you transfer this concept to electromagnetic vibration, when you vibrate with thoughts that have a low-level frequency such as I am unworthy, life is a struggle, others are to blame, and low level emotions such as regret, guilt and fear, then you resonate with, and connect with, other vibrations and waves that are also low on the frequency spectrum. It's like your personal tuner is set to only pick-up low-level frequencies. The opposite is true when your vibration is one of high-level frequencies.

Quantum Physics and The Law of Attraction

I think that the frequency theory of quantum physics explained above is similar to what is meant by the universal Law of Attraction. The Law of Attraction could also be described as the Law of Resonance. We tune into, pick up and connect with the frequencies around us that are vibrating at the same level we are. Conversely, we are unable to tune into frequencies that are at a different spectrum level to that which we are vibrating at.

Your Reticular Activating System
There is an area in the human brain called the Reticular Activating System (RAS). All of your senses except smell (which is wired directly to your brain's emotional centre) connect directly with your RAS. Your RAS filters what sensory information is let into your conscious mind. It prioritises the sensory information that is most important for your conscious mind to be aware of, and decides what sensory input can be safely ignored.

The filters in your RAS are set in a number of ways. There are certain types of information that are hard-wired to be forwarded, such as the sound of your name being called, or anything that threatens your safety or that of your loved ones. Over and above this, the filtering system of your RAS is set according to your current interests, what you decide to pay attention to, and your beliefs. Essentially, your RAS forwards to your conscious mind any sensory evidence that supports what you are focused on or believe. This is probably why, for example, when you are thinking about buying a blue car you begin to notice them all the time. This is also why we are most aware of whatever supports what we believe, and whatever our current dominant thoughts and feelings are. For example, when you feel happy and positive, then your RAS becomes tuned in to notice things that support that, and life seems full of good and happy things. That becomes your perception of reality.

Which Explanation is Correct?
Personally, I believe elements of all of these explanations are correct, and that they fit together as part of a larger picture. Moreover, we do not necessarily need to understand why something works in order to use it to get results. I don't really understand how light-bulbs work, but I use them because I want the outcome they provide. The agreed upon bottom line is that what you focus your thoughts on, draws more of the same into your life. What is important to know, is that you always have the power to choose what you think. To know that no matter what

level you are at now, you can always choose to reach for a better feeling thought, and as you focus on it, evidence to support that better feeling thought will begin to come into your awareness.

The Magic of the Universe
There are people who believe and teach that success comes only through hard work and obsessive effort, and there are people who believe and teach that the law of attraction means that if you focus on what you want and visualize it clearly then the Universe will bring it to you. I think the sweet spot is a balance of both, which you can describe as a balance of masculine and feminine energy (doing and receiving). It is a balance of mindset and practice. Our beliefs shape how we perceive life is. If you believe that you have to hustle, and strive and work harder than others in order to succeed, then that will become how life is for you, and your mind will highlight to you evidence of that being how life is. There are many people who have achieved success this way and therefore teach that this is the way to success based on their experience. However, just because many people have had a particular experience does not mean that it is true, or true for everybody. It is the reality they have created for themselves through their thoughts and beliefs.

Quantum physics is revealing scientifically what spiritual leaders have long taught – that anything is possible with faith and belief. Everything is energy and there are limitless potentialities and possibilities of how life can evolve. Within that, we have the power to choose which potential we want to make into a physical reality. Theoretically, you could believe that all things simply come to you and create that reality for yourself, however, it wouldn't make for a very interesting life. The joy is in the journey; in what we experience and learn, and how we grow and expand as our creations unfold. Moreover, we usually need to grow into a new version of ourselves in order to step into manifesting a new reality. Fulfilment comes from taking inspired action with a sense of being in flow, and of being guided and supported by Universal/divine energy (this may be described by you as God, Source Energy, the quantum field, Spirit Guides, Ancestors or whatever feels true for you).

The belief that success only comes from hard work, is based in working to achieve something from a need to be better and prove yourself. Success can come with ease and flow when you take action to bring a desire to physical fruition from a sense of fullness in yourself that overflows. It is not about how much action you take, the true key to success without stress is the beliefs that underlie the action. The real key is whether or not you feel worthy. If you feel a strong sense of self-worth, then fulfilling success will come with ease and flow. If not, then you will strive and push to earn it.

Focusing on how you can create good feelings for yourself in the present moment/each day also builds your resilience. When you think that you can only feel happy, satisfied, successful or peaceful once you have done or achieved certain things, then challenges and setbacks on the way to manifesting your dreams and desires can feel much more overwhelming (this is also an 'at effect', reactive, conditional way of operating). When your focus is on how you can feel good every day no matter what is going on, then you have an emotional buffer.

Focusing on the feeling and how you can feel that now also helps you to remain more motivated to move forward because the journey is very much part of the goal. It's not just the end achievement that matters, you are experiencing aspects of satisfaction all along the way to the ultimate fulfilment, and you explore into all the ways you can feel the way you want rather than just holding the belief that you need to have or do one certain thing in order to feel satisfied and fulfilled.

Question 2: How do I want to be today? What do I want to embody?

Sit with the feeling/s you wrote down in response to Question one and play with embodying that as your essence today. By play with it I mean don't take it too seriously. Be curious and have fun with it. Ask yourself, "how can I feel and be . . . [emotional essence]? What would that look like? Since I am . . . [emotional essence], how will I speak, move, dress, act . . ? What qualities would I like to cultivate or call-in?

Just as important as the question "What do I want?" is the question, "Who do I need to become to have that?" Create an identity of yourself as the person who has what you want and embody aspects of that each day. For example, if you want to be in a loving, committed relationship you could ask yourself, "Who would I be if I was in a healthy, nourishing, aligned intimate relationship?" If you want to lose weight you could ask yourself, "Who would I be if I was fit and healthy and loved the way my body is?" If you want to be more financially abundant you could ask yourself, "Who would I be if I was financially and materially rich?" I also sometimes include relevant focus statements as part of what I want to embody. For example, "I am frolicking in my joy", or "I am inspired to say things that connect deeply with people."

Write down characteristics of how you would feel and act, and then explore embodying them on a daily basis in whatever way you can. Doing this has two key effects: it aligns you with the energy of what you want, and it focuses you on what you can control. You can always control how you focus your thoughts, how you manage your feelings and how you act. You don't have so much control over how external things manifest in your life. Coach and author Lorinn Krenn frames this as creating a life that is an invitation for what you want to come in. Embodying what you desire in this way shifts you from a hoping and waiting state which drains your energy and gives your power away, to a pro-active, positively creative state. When you are waiting and hoping for something to happen, you are actually in a state of resistance because you don't like where you currently are and you are hoping that something external will happen to change your reality. Another reflection question you can ask is "How can I create a reality that invites in what I desire?"

Question 3: What is most important to me today?

Before you start thinking about all the tasks that you think you need to do, decide what is important to you today. If you are not sure what is important to you then consider what nourishes you, the people you enjoy being with most, the things you most enjoy doing, long-held desires or goals, and what you like in terms of a living or working environment. You may also like to ask yourself: "What do I need most today?" Or, "What is the most loving thing I can do for myself today?" Decide your priorities before you start preparing your schedule for the day.

Step 3: Prioritise

*The key is not to prioritise what's on your schedule,
but to schedule your priorities.*

Steven Covey

When you get up in the morning and just launch into responding
to other people's needs and calls for attention, and doing what
you think needs to be done, it often stimulates feelings of being
rushed and overwhelmed and like there is never enough time. If
you want to feel more fulfilled and happier then do what is truly
important to you first. Let go of being a slave to the urgent. Leave
off reading emails, and social media posts/messages until you
have fed your soul and done what you WANT to do. The rest can
wait. Everything will not fall down. In fact, when you take time
to feed yourself first, everything is more likely to fall into place.

*There is a vitality, a life force, an energy, a quickening that is
translated through you into action, and because there is only one of
you in all time, this expression is unique. And if you block it, it will
never exist through any other medium and will be lost.*

Martha Graham -mind-body wellness and fitness expert

Create a Task Focus List

I like to call a list of action points a task focus list rather than a "to
do" list. "To do" sounds like a command. It has a heavy energy
of effort and responsibility attached to it. Task focus list has an
energy of choice – this is what I want to focus on today. Use a

copy of the Daily Focus Sheet to plan your day. You can print off and use paper copies, or create a digital version. I use Trello to do the brainstorm planning aspects from the Daily Focus Sheet, and then create a schedule on Google Calendar. Use whatever works well for you. The advantage of using a digital calendar is that you can set regular activities as repeating tasks, and you can link in with other digital calendars such as a work one, so that key events automatically show on your personal calendar.

Brainstorm and Prioritise All Your Tasks

In the planning section of the Daily Focus Sheet, write down everything you think you want and need to do. I have separated this into four main life categories to consider. Thinking about tasks for each of these areas will help you to maintain balance in your life:

Personal (physical, mental, spiritual)
Relationships and social
Work and finances
Home creation and maintenance

In the "Personal" section on the Daily Focus Sheet, there is a prompt to write the top three things which are your bliss or that uplift you. When you are doing your planning, plan ways to incorporate aspects of these into every day. I have also included three sub-headings in the personal section: physical, mental and spiritual. These are to prompt you to consider all of these aspects of your personal wellbeing every day. You can interpret "spiritual" in any way that resonates with you in terms of your life-force, soul, or religious or spiritual beliefs. Western culture promotes the belief that productivity determines our value and that we haven't accomplished anything unless we have done active work based tasks. I invite you to see the value and accomplishment in nourishing yourself first so that you can take a step back and see which tasks are the most important to give your time and energy to, and so that you are resourced to give more to them. What if you thought about living your life in terms of managing your energy resources rather than your time resources? How would that shift things for you? For example, would that raise the value of rest for you as a key part of increasing your energy?

Once you have brainstormed all the activities you have in your awareness to do, then colour code each item as being in one of three categories: 'Want to', 'Have to' or 'Should'. Make the 'want to' tasks into your priority for the day – the things that are linked to what is most important to you and to your big picture feeling desires. Give yourself permission to do what you want to do. You are a unique expression of the universe, of Life. If you do not live the fullest version of your authentic self and desires, then something will be blocked and lost, not just for you, but in the expansion of all life. Prioritise your top three "want to" tasks and schedule them into your day first. If you can do them at the start of the day then do so to avoid them getting shunted because your time goes to other things over the course of the day.

Then, look closely at the 'have to' jobs and decide if you do really have to do it, or whether it can be let go, or delegated to someone else (parents, think about things you are doing for your kids that they could be doing for themselves.) Many times, the things we think we "have to" do - we don't really have to. Look at your final "have to" list and prioritise the top three. Focus on getting these done first and then do anything else you have time for. Most of us rarely get through all of our daily to do lists. This way, you know you at least have a good chance of getting the most important things done. I also find that having a clear task list that is prioritised in terms of what is most important to me helps me to be more focused and I am less likely to let days pass by doing 'fluff' tasks and spending hours being distracted.

Completely let go of any tasks you have categorised as "should" (i.e. I should do that). Erase them from your list. Whenever we think we should do something, we are responding to the desires and expectations of other people rather than our own. "Shoulds" are not actually your responsibilities to carry or fulfil. Let them go or assign them to the person who is actually responsible for them. Also be aware that we often create "shoulds" for ourselves based on what we think will please other people.

If other tasks or demands come up over the day, process them through according to these three categories rather than simply reacting to them automatically. Are they a "Want to", a "Have to" or a "Should"? After you have brainstormed all your tasks and prioritised them in terms of want to, have to or should, then you can plan your day on the schedule included on the Daily Focus Sheet, or in a separate paper/electronic diary.

Put first things first – the most important thing, is to keep the most important thing, the most important thing

Jim Kwik

Focus and Decision Enable You to Relax and Trust

When you make meeting your needs a priority, you release the flow of support from the Universe. You'll feel much happier, which is a high vibration emotion, and attracts more high vibration love and joy into your life. Deciding what you want and moving purposefully towards it, sends a clear message for other people and the Universe to respond to. It also helps you to let go of all the tasks and people that don't contribute to that. It can act as a foundation which helps you to release expectations and responsibilities that are not in accordance with your authentic self (usually, these are "should"). Additionally, it simplifies your life, reduces the amount of stress you feel, and opens space for creative flow. Clearing your energy signal of blocking low vibration feelings like resentment, anger, guilt and fear makes it higher more of the time. In other words, you become a better match to manifest what you asked for.

Step 4: Actualise

Take inspired action based on what you decided was the emotional essence you were going to embody today and what is on your prioritised task focus list. I recommend that you don't check your phone or emails until you have checked off at least one of the priorities on your list. This is something American brain coach Jim Kwik does and teaches. Checking social media and emails trains your brain to be distracted and wires your brain to be reactive. In a study done by high performance coach Brendan Burchard, they found that people were on average 30% more productive if they did not check their email or phone messages within the first 60 minutes of their day. You can't be successful and fulfilled if you are giving up your power to something outside of yourself. Your email inbox and social media notifications are other people's priorities imposing on your life. It is your choice whether you react to them or create your life according to your priorities.

The inbox is nothing but a convenient organising system of other people's agendas

Brendan Burchard

Frame Your Day with Gratitude

The last part of actualising your created day is consciously reviewing it with gratitude and noticing how today has been a really good day. I have included some guide questions as the last section of the Daily Focus Sheet titled "End of Day Review." It is best to do this later in the evening just before going to bed and to avoid looking at any technology (news, social media, email, TV) after you have done this. However, if you are going to be socially engaged in the evening then you could do it earlier before you go out. I also like to start my day with pre-emptive gratitude by thanking the Universe for all that I am receiving. When you are working through the review questions, be honest and self-responsible and also self-compassionate. Celebrate what went well, learn from what didn't, and see everything as simply information and feedback to help you live your best life. If anything comes up as a task while you are doing the review, then note it in the planning section of your next day's Daily Focus Sheet.

Appreciation and gratitude focus your awareness into the present and stimulates internal motivation to continue with this practice. This review process is about knowing yourself, not judging yourself. This is not about assessing whether you ticked off everything on your to do list. It is about considering what you experienced today with positive curiosity. Self-reflection with honest and compassionate self-awareness is a key part of living a created life and being "at effect". When you don't self-reflect, you continue living the same patterns, getting the same results and losing vitality.

Gratitude can rewire your brain to deal with circumstances with more awareness and broader perception. It reduces stress and regulates your hypothalamus which helps you to sleep more soundly. Good sleep gives you good energy levels, and good energy levels make it much easier to be proactive about creating your life. Practicing gratitude trains your brain to focus on positive thoughts and emotions more often. What we think about just before we go to sleep, is what is most active in our mind and more likely to be embedded. Thinking about what we love, what we enjoy, what is important to us, and what we feel grateful to have received, just before we go to sleep, means that those things will be dominant in our mind as we drift into sleep, and consolidated to become part of our mental programming.

Start it Slow and Celebrate Your Progress

If you are not used to doing any kind of reflective or planning practice you may like to ease into it. It is better to do one step well and consistently, than to try and do everything, but rush it, or to not do anything because you feel like you can't do it all. Even taking 5-10 minutes in the morning to bring your awareness to your heart and set an intention for a feeling you want to embody for the day can have significant benefit, especially if you do it every day with conscious attention. Doing one part consistently every day is more effective at creating transformation than doing everything once or every so often. The research of BJ Fogg, author of *Tiny Habits*, shows that there are three things that make starting a new habit most effective:

1. Start with one small piece/change at a time that is easy to achieve
2. Attach the new action to something you already routinely do
3. Congratulate yourself and celebrate every small step of your progress

Start where you are and do whatever you think you can do, knowing that if you want your life to change, then you need to do something differently to what you are doing now. Most importantly, notice and celebrate every way in which you show up and move forward.

Appendix 1: Focus Statements & Soul Truths

You can use these sample focus statements to support your core desires and intentions. I prefer to use the term focus statements rather than affirmations as a reminder that they are useful to help set your focus rather than to try and convince or programme yourself in the way that affirmations are sometimes used. You can choose one that feels relevant for you in the moment and set it as a reminder on your phone or write it in your diary. You can also use these focus statements as prompts for doing the five senses visualisation process. As they are more general than your core desire, they can help you move into high-frequency vibrations more easily because you are not as attached to them as you are to your core desire. I invite you to play with these focus statements, to try them on like you are trying on new clothes and playing with having a new identity.

I also call them soul truths because I believe that these statements are the perspective, belief, reality and truth held by your highest self, your soul, the part of you that is part of the divine or quantum field. While these things may not be manifest in your physical reality yet, you can tune into them being true in an energetic sense from the perspective of your soul.

Empowerment

I give myself permission to want and to receive what I want
I can do this and ask for this to honour myself
I am worthy and deserving of all the good that life has to offer
What can be created is unlimited and not constrained by current physical reality.

I am expanding in love, prosperity and positive energy every day
I inspire others
I can feel good about myself
I can make positive changes in my life
I am open and receptive to new opportunities for (income, love, wellbeing) from expected and unexpected sources
I have decided to understand that my emotions are my indicator of my energy frequency
I am choosing to be focused and definite in my purpose
I matter
I love myself /I choose to love myself/I am beginning to love myself/I am getting better and better at loving myself
I am worthy/I choose to begin to know my worthiness
I am valuable
I have great purpose
I radiate beauty
I am worthy of happiness/I am allowed to be happy
I am wise
I am amazing and have all I need to succeed
I am designed for success
I am intelligent
I am growing
I am learning
I am creating and manifesting a better and better life for myself
I choose to find the beauty around me
I choose to honour my desires/I am allowed to have what I want
I can resource myself
I'm discovering talents that I did not know I had
Wonderful new doors are opening for me all the time
I'm in the process of positive changes and I deserve the best
Everything is working out for my highest good
I am safe
I am creating safety within myself
Life is a pathway of awakening and evolving
I choose to think thoughts that create a healthy atmosphere within me and around me

I choose to believe in myself
I choose to believe that I am worthy
I have the power to create and build the life that I desire
Life can be easy
What if this could be easy?
Time expands for me
I am loved
I am experiencing happiness and success in all areas of my life
I am resourceful
I take care of myself
I give myself what I need
I am choosing to show up
I am focusing on my progress
Life is working with me

Love and Relationships
I am worthy and lovable
I radiate love and love fills my life
I am investing in friendships that are uplifting for me
I am investing my time and energy in connecting with people I respect and admire
I am overjoyed to create so much value in all my relationships.
I rejoice in the equality and balance of exchange in all my relationships.
I have so many great and wonderful people in my life
I am safe on my own
I can be happy on my own
I am loved
Love is flowing abundantly to me in all ways

Health and Body
I love and appreciate my body
I honour my body and take good care of it
I allow my body to return to its natural, vibrant health
I accept good health now
I love my body and I support it's wellbeing
I listen to my body

I choose to think thoughts that create a healthy atmosphere within me and around me
I accept my body as my most intimate life partner
My body is worthy of love and respect as it is
I choose to see my own beauty
My body holds and cares for me
Health is wealth

Money, Abundance and Success
Money is the energy of support, appreciation, value and freedom
Money is the root of all freedom
I love money
Money creates the freedom for me to offer my true gifts
I am a money magnet naturally attracting wealth and prosperity into my life every day
I am financially free to live life on my own terms
I am grateful for the infinite circulation of money all around me
I am aligned with the energy and consciousness of abundance
Money flows to me effortlessly in an abundant way
I am financially stable and secure knowing my needs are always met
I am worthy of receiving unlimited wealth and success
I give thanks for all the riches life has to offer
I am a powerful money manifester, money is drawn to me magnetically
New avenues for wealth are opening up to me now in fun and exciting ways
I am continually attracting lucrative opportunities
Abundance is my natural state of being
I am grateful for having multiple streams of income that bring joy and fulfillment into my life
The Universe fully supports me in manifesting prosperity/financial abundance
I am open to receiving financial blessings from unexpected sources
I have unlimited potential to achieve my financial desires
Money flows easily to me from known and unknown sources

Money comes easily to me from expected and unexpected sources
I am continually attracting lucrative opportunities to generously share my gifts with the world
I am grateful for financial freedom and the ability to live life on my own terms
I am financially free to live life on my own terms
I am a conscious creator of wealth and success
I am aligned with the energy of wealth and success
I am open to infinite opportunities for prosperity
I am divinely guided to investments, resources and partnerships for exponential prosperity
I am financially free to focus on my passions and share my gifts
I am open and receptive to unexpected income opportunities
Money flows easily in my life
I am continually attracting lucrative and joyful ways to generate income
New opportunities for income are arising in miraculous and exciting ways
I am continually attracting more wealth and prosperity
It is safe, right and good to have what I want
I am grateful for multiple streams of passive income
I like being in alignment with winning
I like having a perspective of winning that allows me to feel good about winning and allows me to win
I like being in alignment with and feeling good about being first
I like being in alignment with and feeling good about being on top
I love that new things are coming into my life that suit all my needs
I am naturally attracting good fortune
I give myself permission to prosper
Abundance is flowing to me at all times in limitless ways
Money can come to me at any time in any way
I am a powerful creator and I have a limitless supply of money, creativity, love and energy. I attract all the resources I need to thrive.

I am expanding my earning power by creating even more value in what I offer, reaching more people with ease, and making authentic invitations to others for them to participate in and receive my gifts

I save and invest mindfully and give myself the gift of feeling prosperous, ensuring I always have more than enough to give and share.

I live in a field of generosity and connection, knowing I always have a limitless supply and more than enough to give.

I am living in the frequency of success. I am celebrating and feeling good about all success, no matter whose success it is.

I am living in the frequency of abundance. I am celebrating and feeling good about all examples of abundance in my life and life all around me.

As I pay people and companies, I feel appreciation for what they have given me and I bless them with abundance.

When I pay for things, I am supporting the people who work in those businesses. I am blessing people.

I am finding ways to feel good about money flowing through me. I bless people with money.

I am abundantly resourced to give to others. I am a channel for abundance.

I am becoming more confident and wealthier

Appendix 2: Daily Focus Sheet

The questions from the Daily Focus Sheet are listed below. You can access a printable version of the Daily Focus Sheet for free from the Resources page on janinelattimore.com. Alternatively, you can use these questions to plan in your own journal or use them to create a digital version. Personally, I have created a board on Trello with the questions from the Daily Focus Sheet as cards, and then I schedule tasks in Google calendar. I use these options because I can easily access them on my phone or laptop. Please note that although the Daily Focus Sheet has spaces on pages one and two for you to add things to do in each of the four major areas of your life, you do not need to fill in all of the boxes every day. However, I do encourage you to always fill in the "Personal" to-do brainstorm box and to put something under each of the three categories of physical, mental and spiritual. This ensures that you are nourishing all aspects of yourself every day. They don't need to be big things. It could be something as simple as walking up the stairs at work instead of taking the lift, or smiling at yourself in the mirror in the morning and saying "I love you" to yourself. It could be having a nap. Spiritual can be anything that feeds your soul or spirit. That might be tuning into your heart for 5 minutes, or meditating for 15 minutes, or doing something creative like singing or dancing, or it could be praying or some form of religious practice.

This focus sheet is not about mastering every aspect or detail of your life. It is about helping you clarify what is most important to you and making that a priority. It will also help you to identify what is actually your responsibility as opposed to a "should", and where you could ask for help. Focus on 2-3 key things that are most important and which will make the most difference in your life right now. Put those first, and then do anything else you have time and energy for.

I encourage you to take inspired action rather than just doing things to take some form of action. Doing things just for the sake of doing creates busy-ness and stress. It doesn't have the right energy to it. Inspired action is action that you are internally prompted to take when you tune into your desires and what is important to you. When you have strong clarity about what you really want, then ideas of what to do will come to you. If you feel like you are stuck, or fearful or procrastinating, then it could be that you are not stepping into your full or true heart's desire. It could also be a sign that you have underlying subconscious limiting beliefs or emotional wounding, in which case you may need to get some support from a life coach like myself, or another professional who can help you to identify and release them.

Daily Focus Sheet

How do I want to feel today?
How do I want to be today? What do I want to embody?
What is most important to me today?

Brainstorm of Tasks and Actions (list actions/tasks under the headings below)
Top 3 things that give me bliss:
Personal:
  Physical:
  Mental:
  Spiritual:

Relationships and Social:
Work and Finances:
Home Creation and Maintenance:

Daily Schedule (your schedule for the day prioritised in terms of want to and have to)

End of Day Review
What am I feeling in this moment?
What have I enjoyed or found satisfying today?
What did I do that was important to me?
What have I observed or learned about myself today that will help me to grow?
What have I received today?

On the pages that follow are images of the formatted version of the Daily Focus Sheet which can be downloaded for free from the Resources page of janinelattimore.com.

Daily Focus Sheet

Day and Date:

What fun would I like to have today?

How do I want to feel today?

How do I want to be today? What do I want to embody?

What is most important to me today?

Brainstorm of Tasks and Actions

Personal
Top 3 things that give me bliss:
Physical:

Mental:

Spiritual:

Relationships and Social

Work and Finances

Home Creation and Maintenance

Daily Schedule

Today's feeling intention:

TASK FOCUS LIST

- ☐
- ☐
- ☐
- ☐
- ☐
- ☐
- ☐
- ☐
- ☐

TIME TABLE

05:00
06:00
07:00
08:00
09:00
10:00
11:00
12:00
13:00
14:00
15:00
16:00
17:00
18:00
19:00
20:00
21:00
22:00

NOTES

End of Day Review

What am I feeling in this moment?

What have I enjoyed or found satisfying today?

What did I do that was important to me?

What have I observed or learned about myself today that will help me to grow?

What have I received today?

About the Author

Janine Lattimore: Embodiment Coach and Author

A trained teacher and former youth worker and group fitness instructor, I have had an almost life-long passion for mental, emotional and physical health. I have been helping people to learn, grow and navigate life for over 30 years.

My focus is on what gets the most effective results, the most efficiently. That's why I use and teach embodied mindfulness processes because they are the easiest, fastest and most effective way I have come across for people to create change, healing and transformation for themselves. It is very important to me that I practice what I teach.

I am certified as an NLP Practitioner and Coach, a Nia somatic movement instructor, and as a VITA Sex, Love and Relationships Coach working through embodiment modalities. My books include *10 Steps to Happiness*, *How to Make Fear Your Friend*, and *Free to Eat*, which are all available from Amazon and most ebook platforms.

* 9 7 9 8 2 2 4 7 8 3 7 5 5 *